CLIMATE CHANGE: OUR IMPACT ON EARTH

POLLUTION

by

Harriet Brundle

KidHaven PUBLISHING

Published in 2018 by
KidHaven Publishing, an Imprint of Greenhaven Publishing, LLC
353 3rd Avenue
Suite 255
New York, NY 10010

Designer: Drue Rintoul
Editor: Charlie Ogden

Photocredits
Abbreviations: l-left, r-right, b-bottom, t-top, c-center, m-middle.

Front Cover: background – The Clay Machine Gun, bl – Kaspri, t – Igorsky, b – Jag_cz, tl – design56,
tr – 3dfoto, r – Evannovostro. 4tr – Anirut Thailand. 4r – gkuna. 4b – Matt Berger. 4bl – violetblue. 5br –
titoOnz. 6r – Glamorous Images. 6b – Narin Nonthamand. 7tr – ilozavr. 7b – Patrizio Martorana. 8 –
symbiot. 9tr – Chris Hellyar. 9bl – Christian Draghici. 10tr – Kawin168. 10b – PiggingFoto. 11tr – SOMKIET
POOMSIRIPAIBOON. 11b – abutyrin. 12tr – leungchopan. 12b – Ilona Koeleman. 13tr – Ihor Bondarenko.
13bl – Jacqueline Sarratt via https://commons.wikimedia.org/wiki/File:Eristalis_tenax_on_cup.JPG. 13br –
dkidpix. 14tr – Sean Xu. 14b – anuphadit. 15tr – IM_photo. 15b – Phillip Allaway. 16tr – Levent Konuk. 16b –
Gigira. 17tr – Tom Grundy. 17b – Napat. 18tr – Chubykin Arkady. 18b – ESB Professional. 19tr – maradon
333. 20tr – Ondrej Prosicky. 20bl – 360b. 20b – Mikhail Starodubov. 21tr – Tinxi. 21b – Mikhail Kolesnikov.
22tr – Mikhail Kolesnikov. 22b – David Evison. 23b – Milan Petrovic. 24t – jukurae. 24b – Gl0ck. 25tl –
Kaesler Media. 25tr – forestpath. 25b – forest badger. 26b – otomobil. 27t – somsak suwanput. 28t –
wavebreakmedia. 28m – Diego Cervo. 28b – bikeriderlondon. 29t – kay roxby. 29m – Poznyakov. 29b –
stefanolunardi. Images are courtesy of Shutterstock.com, with thanks to Getty Images, Thinkstock Photo,
and iStockphoto.

Cataloging-in-Publication Data

Names: Brundle, Harriet.
Title: Pollution / Harriet Brundle.
Description: New York : KidHaven Publishing, 2018. | Series: Climate change: our impact on Earth |
Includes index.
Identifiers: ISBN 9781534524712 (pbk.) | 9781534524453 (library bound) | ISBN 9781534524729 (6
pack) | ISBN 9781534524460 (ebook)
Subjects: LCSH: Pollution–Juvenile literature. | Refuse and refuse disposal–Juvenile literature. |
Climatic changes–Juvenile literature.
Classification: LCC TD176.B77 2018 | DDC 363.73–dc23

Printed in the United States of America

CPSIA compliance information: Batch #CW18KL: For further information contact Greenhaven Publishing LLC, New York, New York at 1-844-317-7404.

Please visit our website, www.greenhavenpublishing.com. For a free color catalog of all our
high-quality books, call toll free 1-844-317-7404 or fax 1-844-317-7405.

CONTENTS

Words in **bold** are explained in the glossary on page 31.

WHAT IS CLIMATE CHANGE?

KEY TERMS

- The <u>weather</u> is the day-to-day changes we see and feel outside. For example, the weather may be sunny in the morning and rainy in the afternoon.

- The <u>climate</u> is the usual weather in a place over a longer period of time. For example, Antarctica has an extremely cold climate for most of the year.

- <u>Climate change</u> is the long-term change in the climate and usual weather patterns of an area. Climate change generally affects large areas. It could be a change in the amount of rainfall or the average temperature of an area.

Earth's climate is always changing. Over the last 4.5 billion years, Earth has experienced both hot and cold periods. For the last 11,000 years, Earth's climate has stayed at a stable temperature of around 57°F (14°C). However, in recent years this average temperature has been slowly increasing.

Tropical Climate

Arctic Climate

Why Might a Climate Change?

There are many different reasons for why a climate might change.

Some climate changes throughout history have had natural causes, such as **volcanic eruptions**. However, research has shown that changes to the climate in recent years have not been entirely related to natural causes. It is thought that a process called global warming is largely responsible.

1 Humans use energy for many different reasons, for example, to power cars and light bulbs. This energy is largely produced by burning coal, oil, and natural gas. Together, these things are known as **fossil fuels**. When these fossil fuels are burned, they release many different gases, which are known as "greenhouse gases." Possibly the worst of these greenhouse gases is carbon dioxide.

2 Earth's **atmosphere** is a collection of different gases that surround the planet. The atmosphere allows light and heat from the sun to pass through to Earth. This makes the planet warm. After this, some of the light and heat from the sun bounce off Earth, travel back through Earth's atmosphere, and go into outer space.

3 Greenhouse gases mix with the gases in Earth's atmosphere and stop the heat from the sun bouncing back into outer space. Because of this, the heat gets trapped inside Earth's atmosphere. As a result, the temperature on Earth is rising. The more greenhouse gases that are released into Earth's atmosphere, the hotter Earth will become.

WHAT IS POLLUTION?

*When a harmful substance is added to an **environment** and it causes **negative** effects, it is called pollution.*

Examples of pollution include making streams and rivers dirty and putting harmful **chemicals** into the air. Harmful chemicals and substances that can cause pollution are known as pollutants. There are many different types of pollution, including air pollution, water pollution, noise pollution, and soil pollution. Any type of pollution can be dangerous. Pollution affects animals and plants all around the world, it helps to speed up climate change, and it has been shown to cause illness in humans.

There are two main types of pollution. The first type of pollution includes pollution from things such as factories, pipes, and ships. The **source** of these types of pollution can be traced back to a single place, for example, the individual pipe, factory, or ship. We call this type of pollution "point source pollution," as we know exactly where the pollution came from. Since we know the exact source for these types of pollution, it is easier for us to work out how much damage the pollution will have on the environment. The second type of pollution, called "nonpoint source pollution," is pollution that cannot be traced back to a single source. Nonpoint source pollution happens when rainwater gathers many different pollutants together in the same place, usually in a river or an ocean.

Fumes from factories are one of the biggest sources of air pollution.

These tunnels are a type of point source pollution.

Humans have been causing pollution for a long time. At first, there weren't enough humans to cause too much damage, but that quickly changed. As the number of people on the planet increased, the amount of pollution being caused by humans also increased. Today, many people on the planet own a car, resulting in there being more than 1 billion cars worldwide. If you also think about how many people eat food from plastic containers or use trains or buses to get around, you can see that most people help to pollute the planet every single day. Due to these actions, it is no surprise that humans are causing a lot of pollution and are helping to speed up the effects of climate change and global warming.

It is important that we all try to pollute as little as possible in order to reduce the effects of climate change.

Pollution can be measured in many different ways.

AIR POLLUTION

Air pollution is when pollutants are added into Earth's atmosphere. One cause of air pollution is the burning of fossil fuels, which gives off a gas called carbon dioxide. Carbon dioxide is known as a "greenhouse gas," meaning that large amounts of it in our atmosphere cause global warming.

There are natural causes of air pollution, such as the smoke from fires and the dust that is blown into the air by the wind. Another natural cause of air pollution is the gas released by farm animals called methane. There have always been greenhouse gases in Earth's atmosphere. It was only after humans started adding more pollutants and greenhouse gases into the air that global warming became a problem. Having small amounts of these gases in the atmosphere is natural; it is only when huge amounts of these gases are being released that our atmosphere becomes dangerously polluted.

AIR POLLUTION HAS BEEN PROVEN TO BE HARMFUL TO HUMANS. EXPERTS BELIEVE THAT AIR POLLUTION KILLS OVER 5 MILLION PEOPLE EVERY YEAR.

Cows release methane into the atmosphere.

Air pollution also causes acid rain. When fossil fuels are burned, different harmful gases build up in the atmosphere. As the gases build up, they mix with water droplets to create acid rain. Acid rain can damage buildings, cars, and the **habitats** of plants and animals. When acid rain falls onto cars or buildings, it can be strong enough to badly damage them. When it falls on a natural habitat, such as a forest, it can lead to the deaths of plants and animals.

This building has been damaged by acid rain.

If acid rain falls into lakes, it can be dangerous for the animals and plants that live there and can damage the lake's **ecosystem**.

SOIL POLLUTION

Soil pollution happens when harmful chemicals enter soil. The main cause of soil pollution is powerful and harmful chemicals. Strong chemicals used by factories are sometimes dumped into fields instead of being properly thrown away. Other times, places where garbage is taken, such as landfills, become too full. As the waste overflows, harmful chemicals can leak into the soil.

Another major cause of soil pollution is **pesticides**. Pesticides are chemicals sprayed by farmers onto their **crops.** The pesticides stop insects, mice, and birds from eating the crops. As the farmers spray the pesticides, some of the chemicals also enter the soil. Once they have entered the soil, the pesticides can stay there for a long time. When the soil is used again, any crops that are grown in it will probably contain the chemicals that were in the pesticides.

Landfills can become too full and cause soil pollution.

Soil pollution also has harmful effects on the environment. Plants and trees absorb the carbon dioxide that is released when fossil fuels are burned. In return they give off oxygen, which all animals, including humans, need to survive. If soil becomes too polluted, plants and trees will not be able to grow in it. If fewer plants and trees grew, less carbon dioxide would be taken out of the atmosphere. This would help to speed up the effect of climate change. If the soil stays polluted for a long time, it could mean that trees and plants are never able to grow in it again.

Although soil pollution can be difficult to control, different **organizations** around the world are trying to create new laws that will help to reduce soil pollution. Some people, however, disagree with these laws. This is partly because, for some companies, reducing the amount of pollution they produce would be expensive.

Plant life often dies as a result of soil pollution.

WATER POLLUTION

Water pollution generally occurs when pollutants are released into large areas of water, such as rivers or lakes. There are not many ways in which water pollution can be caused naturally, meaning that nearly all of the polluted water in the world is the fault of humans.

Water covers over 70 percent of the earth's surface, and all plants and animals need it to survive. As the number of people living on the planet has increased, the amount of clean water has become smaller, which has been made worse by pollution. When water pollution is caused by a point source, such as a pipe that releases chemicals into a lake, it is easy for us to see how much damage it causes. For example, if fewer animals have been drinking out of the lake since the pipe started dumping chemicals into it, it is easy to work out that this was caused by the chemicals. Nonpoint source pollution in rivers and lakes happens when rainwater gathers up many different pollutants and dumps them all into the same body of water.

polluted water

point source pollution

When chemicals are washed off the land and into bodies of water, it can cause an increase in the amount of **algae** that grows on the surface of the water. The algae creates a thick layer on top of the water, which stops sunlight getting through. This causes plants that are growing under the water to die. Without these plants, many of the animals that live in or near the water also cannot survive, meaning that the entire ecosystem could be destroyed.

Water pollution is particularly dangerous because it can spread to new places, even to other countries. As the polluted water moves through different channels, such as the ocean, it reaches other countries and causes damage to environments there as well.

algae

rat-tailed maggot

Animals are often used to see how polluted a body of water is. Some insects, such as mayflies, are typically only found near clean water, whereas rat-tailed maggots can happily live in polluted water.

mayfly

13

LIGHT POLLUTION

Light pollution is when lots of man-made light makes the night sky much brighter than it should be. Nowadays, towns and cities are lit up all night by street lamps, car headlights, and lights in homes.

One of the main causes of light pollution is large venues, such as sporting arenas, which often use several lights during the night. When people live close together in a town or a city and use lights during the night, it often causes the sky to glow. This is known as "sky glow," and many people do not like that it makes it hard to see the stars and the moon in the night sky.

Shown here is a stadium in New Orleans.

Mercedes-Benz Superdome

RECENT STUDIES SUGGEST THAT AROUND 80 PERCENT OF PEOPLE CURRENTLY LIVE UNDER SKY GLOW.

sky glow in Bangkok, Thailand

When we turn on a light, it uses electricity. Most electricity is generated by burning fossil fuels, which harms the environment. It is estimated that 15 million tons of carbon dioxide, a harmful greenhouse gas, is produced every year in the United States just so that people can power their outside lights.

Hundreds of years ago, the nights on Earth were dark. As Earth's population grew, we started to use more lights, and the nights in many places stopped being dark. This has had a huge impact upon animals that rely upon darkness. The darkness of night tells animals when they should be asleep and also offers cover from predators. Animals that hunt for their food during the night also need the darkness so that they are not seen by the animals that they are trying to catch. Animals that move to new places at different times of the year, such as birds, sometimes begin their journeys too early or too late because they are confused by man-made lights.

New York City

This leopard is hunting during the night.

GARBAGE

Pollution from garbage covers everything from children dropping candy wrappers in the park to giant pits in the ground being filled in by huge amounts of garbage. A landfill site is a large pit in the ground that gets filled up with garbage. A lot of the garbage that we produce each day is taken away and put into these landfill sites. Landfill sites are used because they contain the garbage in a very small area and keep it away from places where people live. However, there are often chemicals in garbage, and these end up polluting the areas around landfill sites.

After we throw our garbage away, it begins to break down into the different chemicals and substances that it is made from. This is called decomposing. When garbage starts to decompose, chemicals in the garbage are released into the air and soil around the landfill sites.

One of the most harmful types of garbage is plastic. A large amount of plastic is making its way into the ocean, and this is having a very negative effect on the ocean's ecosystems. Animals often mistake the plastic for food and eat it. When they do this, the plastic can damage their **internal organs** and can even cause them to die. Plastic packaging, such as that used to hold drink cans, can become stuck around an animal's beak or nose and cause the animal to starve. There are also many other types of garbage that can trap or injure animals, such as old fishing nets, tin cans, and shards of glass.

Animals often mistake plastic for food.

Over time, the garbage in oceans breaks down into small pieces. It can then be eaten by small animals in the ocean, such as plankton. When these animals are eaten by bigger animals, the damage and impact of eating the plastic is passed on.

THERE ARE 13,000 TINY PIECES OF PLASTIC IN EVERY 0.4 SQUARE MILE (1 SQ. KM) OF OCEAN.

plankton

LONG-TERM EFFECTS OF
POLLUTION

The impact of pollution must be taken seriously, since it is having a range of long-term effects on the environment. While every type of pollution has negative effects, two of the most dangerous types of pollution are air and water pollution. Air and water pollution have already been shown to affect people's health, and it is now known that air pollution is a major cause of global warming and climate change.

Air pollution affects people's health.

We need water to survive. This means that the water on Earth must be looked after so that people continue to have clean water to drink in the future. If the water on planet Earth keeps being polluted, soon there might not be enough clean water to drink.

Pollution also impacts climate change, and climate change causes more extreme weather. For some parts of the world, severe **droughts** are becoming increasingly common. Droughts kill the plant life that humans and animals need for food. As a result, areas with many droughts often become **uninhabitable**.

Climate change is affecting and changing environments too quickly for the animals and plants that live in the environments to keep up. If Earth's average temperature rises by as little as 2.68°F (2°C), up to 30 percent of all the animals and plants on the planet will be at risk of **extinction**.

SINCE 1880, THE TEMPERATURE ON EARTH HAS RISEN BY AROUND 1.7°F (1°C).

SAVING ANIMAL HABITATS

The World Wide Fund for Nature (WWF) is an organization that began in 1961. The organization works to save animals and their habitats from damage and pollution. WWF focuses on many different areas, including the protection of animals and the reduction of climate change. With millions of supporters worldwide and work being carried out in over 100 countries, the WWF is the largest organization of its type in the world.

WWF has done a lot of work based around the pollution from airplanes. Pollution from airplanes is one of the fastest growing sources of greenhouse gases, and the problem is getting worse every year. The WWF is currently working with the International Civil Aviation Organization (ICAO), and they are hoping to reduce the pollution created by airplanes in the future.

© ® WWF

There are many other organizations, such as Greenpeace, The Nature Conservancy, and Natural Resources Defense Council, that work to reduce pollution all around the world. In 2016, Greenpeace began its Detox campaign, which involved companies removing chemicals from their products that are harmful to the environment.

Greenpeace volunteers

National parks and reserves have been set up all over the world to offer a safe place for animals to live. These areas of land are protected by law, meaning that the parks and reserves cannot be damaged by pollution or any other kind of human activity. Other areas, such as the Great Barrier Reef in Australia, are also covered by laws that protect the area by helping to stop pollution. Some parks and reserves offer the opportunity for visitors to pay money to see the animals living there. This money is often used to make sure that the parks stay safe and free from pollution.

Yosemite National Park

THE ARCTIC

Air pollution has caused the temperature on Earth to rise. This rise in temperature has had damaging effects on the North and South Poles. The warmer temperatures have caused large pieces of ice around the North and South Poles to melt. For animals such as polar bears, which have to catch their food on land, less ice makes it much harder for them to survive.

The melting ice is also adding more water into the ocean. This has caused sea levels to rise. As sea levels continue to rise, beaches around the world will begin to be covered by water. Animals that lay their eggs on beaches, such as turtles, will then have to find somewhere else to make their nests.

polar bear

Turtles lay their eggs on beaches.

Greenland is a country in the Atlantic Ocean that has extreme cold often as low as 18°F (-8°C). Greenland is home to a large range of different plants and wildlife, including polar bears, arctic foxes, and reindeer. Around 80 percent of Greenland is covered in a large sheet of ice, making it the second largest area of ice in the world. People only live in the small parts of the country that are not covered in ice.

Greenland

IT'S ESTIMATED THAT 80 PERCENT OF GREENLAND IS COVERED IN ICE. THAT'S OVER 656,000 MILLION SQUARE MILES (1.7 MILLION SQ KM) OF ICE!

The Greenland ice sheet is at risk of melting. Small rises in Earth's temperature are having a huge effect on the ice sheet. Each year, the size of the ice sheet is becoming increasingly smaller. As the ice sheet melts, the sea level rises, and the animals that inhabit Greenland have increasingly less land to live on.

the Greenland ice sheet

OIL SPILLS

When **crude oil** is accidentally released into an environment, it is known as an oil spill. The most damaging oil spills typically occur in the ocean. These are known as marine oil spills. Oil spills often come from tankers, which are big ships that transport crude oil from **offshore** **platforms**. When a marine oil spill occurs, it is difficult to clean up. Oil is lighter than water, meaning that it floats on the surface of the ocean. As the oil spreads out, it creates a thin layer, which is almost impossible to clean up.

Oil is thick and sticky, and it can make it difficult for birds to fly if it gets on their wings. Also, if oil gets into an animal's fur, the fur cannot keep the animal warm, making it easier for them to die from being too cold.

One of the largest oil spills in history happened in 2010 in the Gulf of Mexico, which is a large area of water to the east of Mexico. It was caused by a large explosion in an oil well over 0.6 mile (1 km) below the surface of the ocean. The explosion killed 11 people and injured many more. Following the explosion, oil spilled out into the ocean for 87 days.

The oil spread over 568 miles (915 km) into the surrounding area and caused huge amounts of damage. Despite work to reduce the impact of the disaster, it is thought that thousands of birds and other **species** of animals, such as fish and sea turtles, were killed as a result. It is still unknown how bad the damage was and how it will affect the planet years from now.

Oil can damage a bird's feathers.

the Gulf of Mexico

Austin
Houston
New Orleans
Tallahassee
Tampa
Miami
Havanna
Mérida
Puebla
Veracruz

N

REDUCING POLLUTION

Now that humans are more aware of the dangers and effects of pollution, more is being done to reduce the amount of pollution that is produced by humans. One way of reducing pollution is by using renewable energy. Renewable energy often does not release pollutants, and it is collected from sources that will never run out. One of the most popular sources of renewable energy is the wind. Wind **turbines** have long blades that are pushed by the energy of the wind. As they move, energy is collected that can then be used to power homes, factories, and street lights.

Electric cars are also becoming more popular. These cars run on batteries rather than gasoline. Running a car on gasoline releases many pollutants into the atmosphere, including carbon dioxide, but electric cars do not release any pollutants.

wind turbine

This electric car is recharging.

In an attempt to reduce the amount of garbage being sent to landfill sites, many items are now recyclable. This means that the materials that were used to make the item can be used again and again, rather than being thrown away. For example, drink cans can be melted down so that the metal that they are made out of, called aluminium, can be used again to make more drink cans. It can take as little as six weeks for drink cans to be recycled and put back into shops after they have been put into a recycling bin. If we can reduce the amount of waste being taken to landfill sites, then our air, water, and soil will all be less polluted.

These aluminium cans are being taken to a recycling center.

Laws about pollution have been introduced in most countries around the world in an effort to control the amount pollution that is being produced. Many countries are now setting goals to reduce their pollution in the future. The countries that are currently contributing the most to climate change are China, the United States, Brazil, and Japan. It is important that all countries continue to work toward using renewable energy and reducing the amount of pollutants that they put into the environment if we want to stop the effects of climate change.

HOW CAN WE HELP?

There are many different ways that we can all help to reduce pollution and stop global warming.

 **1** Get involved in any groups or organizations in your local area that are trying to reduce pollution. Use the Internet to discover what other people are doing to help, and see if you would like to join them.

Tell your family and friends about climate change and how important it is to look after our planet. Also, try to get as many people as you can interested in stopping damage to our planet. **2**

 **3** Recycle! It is important that we recycle as much as possible in order to reduce the amount of waste being put into landfill sites. Recycling can be done at home, at school, and in the wider community, so try to make sure that anything you can recycle is taken to special recycling banks or is put in recycling bins.

4 Try not to be wasteful. Food waste also contributes to the waste being dumped in landfill sites, so try to reuse anything that doesn't need to be thrown away, and make sure that food is eaten before it goes out of date.

Try to reduce the amount of fossil fuels that you use. Rather than using the car, try to walk or ride your bike to where you need to go. If you have to use a car, try sharing with others who are also going to the same place. You could also turn down the heating at home and wear more layers of clothing to stay warm instead.

5

6 Plant a tree! Trees absorb some of the greenhouse gases that cause climate change and give off oxygen. The more trees that are planted, the better!

The WWF holds "Earth Hour" every year. On the last Saturday in March, everyone who is taking part turns off the lights in their house for one hour between 8:30 p.m. and 9:30 p.m. The WWF hopes that this act will show how much people care about the planet. Why not join in and turn off your lights for an hour?

USEFUL WEBSITES

Find out about the work of the World Wide Fund for Nature (WWF) and what they are doing to reduce pollution levels at www.worldwildlife.org/threats/pollution.

Use this interactive map to find out how much light pollution there is in your area: cires.colorado.edu/artificial-sky.

To learn how to measure the light pollution in your area yourself, check out this helpful page: darksky.org/light-pollution/measuring-light-pollution.

Take a look at ocean.nationalgeographic.com/ocean to find out more about looking after the world's oceans.

Visit www.nature.org and go to the "where we work" section to find out about conservation work that's happening in your area.

 Go to www.earthtimes.org for interesting blogs and pages that are filled with environmentally friendly ideas and tips.

GLOSSARY

algae	living things that are like plants, but have no roots, stems, leaves, or flowers
atmosphere	the mixture of gases that make up the air and surround Earth
chemical	matter that is mixed with other matter to create changes and is often man-made
crop	a plant such as a grain, vegetable, or fruit that is grown in large amounts
crude oil	naturally occurring oil found deep underground, which is used to make fossil fuels, plastics, and other materials
drought	a long period of little rainfall, which leads to a lack of water
ecosystem	all the living things in an area and how they affect each other
environment	the natural world
extinction	when every member of a species is no longer alive
fossil fuel	a fuel such as gas, coal, and oil that was formed underground millions of years ago from the remains of animals and plants
habitat	a natural environment in which animals or plants live
internal organ	a part inside the body that does a specific job, such as the heart and lungs
negative	something bad or undesirable
offshore platform	a large structure out in the sea that drills deep to find fossil fuels
organization	a group of people who work together with a shared purpose
pesticide	a chemical used to kill animals and insects that damage crops
predator	an animal that hunts other animals for food
source	the place where something comes from
species	a group of very similar animals or plants that are capable of producing young together
turbine	a machine with large blades
uninhabitable	not suitable to live in
volcanic eruption	the natural event that happens when steam and other material violently leaves a volcano

INDEX